Bright Beginnings

ILLUSTRATED BIBLE STORIES FOR YOUNG HEARTS

FREE

Book

Unlock Your Free Bonus Book!

As a heartfelt **thank you** for choosing our book, we're delighted to offer you a **FREE book.**

Table of Contents

The Little Lost Sheep

Luke 15:3-7

Once upon a time, nestled in a field full of soft, green grass, there lived a loving shepherd with his big flock of 100 woolly sheep. Every day, the shepherd counted his sheep, "1, 2, 3..." all the way to 100, to make sure all his fluffy friends were safe.

One bright, sunny day, as he finished counting, he realized with a gasp, "I only count 99! One of my little sheep is missing!" His heart pounded like a drum. But the shepherd, brave and kind, decided to leave his 99 safe sheep and start an exciting quest to find his lost little sheep.

Over towering mountains he journeyed, through playful rivers he waded, and into shadowy woods he ventured. He called, "Little Sheep, where are you?" But the little sheep was nowhere to be found. Still, the shepherd didn't lose hope. His love for the little sheep was bigger than the biggest mountain.

Finally, after a long and tiring day, behind a giant, sturdy rock, he found his frightened little sheep. Seeing its shepherd, the sheep's eyes twinkled like morning dew, and it bleated with joy. The shepherd's heart filled with happiness as he carefully lifted the tiny sheep into his warm, protective arms.

With the little sheep safely tucked on his shoulders, the shepherd returned home under a sky painted with vibrant sunset colors. He gathered all his friends and neighbors, declaring with a bright smile, "Rejoice with me, my friends! I have found my lost sheep!" Everyone danced and sang, their hearts filled with joy, under the sparkling blanket of stars.

This magical story reminds us of a very special love: the love God has for each one of us. Just like the shepherd who searched for the little lost sheep, if we ever feel lost, scared, or alone, God is always there to find us and bring us back to safety. No matter how big the world might seem, or how small we might feel, we are incredibly precious to God, and He will always look out for us. Remember, even if you feel like a tiny sheep in a big, big world, in God's loving eyes, you are the most important part of His grand adventure.

Daniel and the Lion

Daniel 6:16-24

In a time long, long ago, there was a brave and good man named Daniel. Daniel was special because he always tried to do what was right and prayed to God every day.

Daniel lived in a kingdom where the king was tricked into making a law that said nobody could pray to anyone except the king. But Daniel knew this was wrong, so he kept praying to God.

Some people didn't like Daniel because he was so good, so they told the king that Daniel had broken the new law. The king was very sad because he liked Daniel, but he had to obey his own law. So, Daniel was put in a den with big, scary lions!

Now, you'd think this would be the end for Daniel, but guess what? Daniel was not scared. He trusted in God and knew he was not alone.

That night, God sent an angel to shut the mouths of the lions. Instead of being fierce and dangerous, the lions became friendly! They didn't hurt Daniel at all. They became his companions for the night, purring and laying down next to him.

In the morning, the king hurried to the lions' den, and he was overjoyed to see Daniel safe and sound! He realized that Daniel's God was the true God and made a new law that everyone should respect Daniel's God.

Just like Daniel in the lion's den, sometimes we might feel scared when things go wrong, or when people don't understand us. But remember, God is always with us and can turn scary situations into safe ones. Trusting in what's right and having faith can turn even lions into friends. And remember, it's always important to do what you know is right, even when others don't agree.

David and Goliath

I Samuel 17

In the rolling green hills of Bethlehem, there lived a young shepherd boy named David. Even though he was small, David had a heart full of courage and a spirit as bright as the sun.

One day, a big problem arose. A giant named Goliath, as tall as a tree and as tough as a boulder, challenged the Israelites to send out a warrior to fight him. The bravest soldiers were afraid and dared not face Goliath.

But David was not afraid. He decided to stand up to Goliath, not with a sword or armor, but with his trusty slingshot and five smooth stones from a stream. His brothers were worried, "You're too small," they said. But David just smiled and said, "With God's help, I can do big things."

David approached Goliath, who laughed at him, "Am I a dog that you come at me with sticks?" But David didn't let Goliath's words scare him. He answered boldly, "You come against me with sword and spear, but I come against you in the name of the Lord."

With a deep breath, David put a stone in his slingshot and, with a whoosh, sent it flying. The stone hit Goliath right in the forehead. The mighty giant stumbled and fell down with a thud that shook the earth.

The soldiers cheered, and the Israelites celebrated their victory. David, the little shepherd boy, had defeated the giant! His courage and faith had saved his people.

The story of David and Goliath teaches us that no matter how small we are or how big the problems seem, with faith and courage, we can overcome them. Just like David defeated Goliath with a small stone and a big heart, we too can face our challenges bravely. And remember, it doesn't matter how small or young you are, with God's help, you can do big things! So, hold onto your courage, keep faith in your heart, and always believe in yourself. You are stronger than you think!

Jonah and the Big Fish

Jonah 1-2

In a vibrant city bustling with life, there lived a man named Jonah. One day, God spoke to Jonah, "Go to the great city of Nineveh and tell the people to be kind and good." But Jonah felt a flutter of fear in his heart and, instead of heading to Nineveh, he sneakily boarded a ship sailing in the opposite direction.

As the ship glided across the mighty ocean, a monstrous storm erupted! Waves crashed onto the ship like giant watery fists, the wind howled like a hundred angry wolves, and the sky was as dark as a raven's feather. The sailors were terrified! They found Jonah snoozing soundly and woke him up, "Pray to your God, maybe He will calm this storm!" they cried.

Jonah, feeling a heavy thud in his heart, knew this was all because he didn't listen to God. He faced the sailors, "Throw me into the sea," he said bravely, "and the storm will stop." And so, with a gulp and a prayer, they did, and miraculously, the sea became as calm as a glassy lake.

Suddenly, up from the deep waters came a fish so enormous it could have been a mountain! It swallowed Jonah in one giant gulp! Inside the fish's belly, Jonah found himself in a world of dark, swirling water. He realized he had made a big mistake by running away. So, Jonah prayed to God for help, promising to do as God asked if he was saved.

After three days and nights, the colossal fish gave a mighty belch and spat Jonah out onto a sandy beach. Jonah, thankful and a little soggy, scrambled to his feet and without delay, he went to Nineveh. He shared God's message and the people listened, changed their ways, and the city was saved!

Now, little ones, Jonah's adventure teaches us that even when we're scared, it's important to listen and do what's right. And if we make mistakes, like Jonah, we should admit them and ask for forgiveness. Remember, no matter how big our errors are, God's love and forgiveness are even bigger! Just like Jonah got a second chance, we too can learn, grow, and make things right. Always remember, it's never too late to turn around and choose the right path.

The Mustard Seed

Matthew 13:31-32

Once upon a time, in a cozy little village, there lived a wise woman named Ruth. Ruth had the tiniest treasure, a mustard seed. This seed was so tiny it could easily disappear in the palm of her hand!

One bright, sunny day, Ruth decided to plant this teeny, tiny mustard seed in her garden. She dug a little hole in the rich, chocolate-brown earth, dropped in the seed, and covered it gently with soil. Every day, she would water it and sing to it under the glowing sun and whispering wind.

Days passed into weeks, and the little seed remained hidden beneath the earth. Ruth's friends would sometimes ask, "Why do you take care of that tiny seed? It's so small, what can it become?" But Ruth simply smiled and said, "Just wait and see."

And then, one magical morning, a tiny green sprout pushed through the soil. It was so small, but Ruth knew it was the start of something wonderful. Each day, it grew a little more, reaching up towards the big blue sky. Weeks turned into months, and the sprout grew and grew. It became a plant, then a bigger plant, and then a grand tree, taller than Ruth, her house, and even some of the small hills nearby! Its branches spread out like open arms, and its leaves danced joyfully in the wind.

The tiny mustard seed had grown into the biggest tree in the village! Birds from near and far came to build their nests, and the children of the village played under its cool shade. Ruth's friends were amazed, "How could something so tiny become so big?" They marveled at the mustard tree, now a centerpiece of their lovely village.

Ruth's tiny mustard seed teaches us that even the smallest things can grow into something amazing. You may feel small now, but just like the mustard seed, you are filled with incredible potential. Remember, it doesn't matter how small you start. With care, patience, and time, you, too can grow and achieve great things. Always have faith in your own potential, just like Ruth had faith in her tiny mustard seed. Because within every tiny beginning, there lies the promise of a beautiful, grand tree.

Strong Samson

Judges 13-16

Once upon a time, in a land far away, there was a man named Samson. Samson was known all around because he was the strongest man in the world! And do you know what his secret was? His long, long hair. God had given Samson this strength, and as long as his hair wasn't cut, he was stronger than anyone else.

One day, Samson fell in love with a woman named Delilah. But some mean people came to Delilah. They wanted to know Samson's secret and promised her lots of money if she could find it out.

So Delilah asked Samson, "What makes you so strong?" At first, Samson didn't tell her the truth. But after she asked him many, many times, Samson finally told her about his hair.

While Samson was sleeping, Delilah called the mean people. They cut off his hair, and when he woke up, Samson had lost all his strength. The mean people were able to capture him and they even took away his ability to see.

But as time passed, Samson's hair began to grow back. And with his hair, his strength returned too. One day, while the mean people were celebrating, they brought Samson to show everyone that they had captured him.

Samson prayed to God, asking for his strength one last time. He pushed against the pillars that held the building, and with his great strength, he knocked them down. The building fell, and all the mean people inside were defeated.

Just like Samson, we may have special gifts that make us unique and strong, but true strength comes from God. It's important to be careful about who we trust and to always remember that even when things go wrong, if we turn to God, He can give us the strength to face our challenges.

Joseph and His Colorful Coat

Genesis 37-45

Once upon a time, in a land filled with sand and sun, lived a young boy named Joseph. Joseph was special because he had eleven brothers, but he was the most loved by his father, Jacob. To show his love, Jacob gave Joseph a beautiful coat of many colors. It was the most colorful coat anyone had ever seen!

Joseph's brothers saw this coat and were very jealous. They didn't like that their father loved Joseph the most. One day, Joseph had a dream. In his dream, he saw eleven sheaves of wheat bowing down to his sheaf. He told his brothers about his dream. "This means that one day, you will all bow down to me," said Joseph.

This made his brothers even more jealous. One day, when Joseph was far from home, his brothers took his colorful coat and sold him to people going to Egypt. They told their father that a wild animal had taken Joseph.

In Egypt, Joseph was put in jail. But he didn't lose hope. He knew that he could understand dreams, a gift from God. Soon, the Pharaoh, the ruler of Egypt, heard about Joseph's gift. He had been having dreams that no one could understand. Joseph was brought to Pharaoh and he explained his dreams. "There will be seven years of plenty of food, followed by seven years of famine," Joseph said. Pharaoh was so impressed that he made Joseph a ruler in Egypt, second only to him.

Years later, when the famine came, Joseph's brothers came to Egypt to buy food. They didn't recognize Joseph, but he recognized them. They bowed to him, just like in Joseph's dream. Joseph forgave his brothers and they were reunited.

Just like Joseph, sometimes we might face difficult times, and people might be unkind because they are jealous or don't understand us. But we should always remember to stay hopeful and make the most of our unique gifts. Even when things seem bad, God has a plan for us. And, like Joseph, we should always be ready to forgive and show kindness, even to those who have wronged us.

The Tower of Babel

Genesis 11:1-9

Once upon a time, long, long ago, all the people in the world spoke the same language. They understood each other perfectly. There were no misunderstandings or miscommunications because everyone's words sounded the same.

As the people moved to the east, they found a place called Babylonia and decided to settle there. They said to each other, "Let's make bricks and build a city with a tower that reaches to the sky. This will make us famous and keep us from being scattered all over the world."
They worked day and night, stacking brick upon brick, building their tower higher and higher. The tower seemed like it could touch the sky!
But God saw what the people were doing. They were not building the tower to honor Him but to make themselves famous. They were also trying to stay together in one place, when God had told them to spread out and fill the earth.

So, God decided to mix up their language. Suddenly, people couldn't understand each other anymore. One person would say one thing, but the other person heard something completely different! It was all very confusing.

With all the misunderstanding, the people couldn't work together to build the tower anymore. They began to move away and scatter all over the world, just as God had originally intended. This place came to be known as Babel, which means "confusion."

The story of the Tower of Babel teaches us that we should not try to make ourselves great without God. We should always remember to work together and use our abilities to do good things that please God, not just to make ourselves famous. And even when things don't go as planned, we should remember that God has a bigger plan for us. It's important to listen to God's words and follow His guidance in our lives.

Balaam's Surprise Teacher

Numbers 22:21-34

In a colorful kingdom, there lived a wise man named Balaam. Balaam had a gray donkey, who was his faithful friend and companion on many adventures. The donkey was quiet and gentle, with soft, loving eyes.

One sunny morning, Balaam saddled up his donkey for a journey. They traveled through valleys painted with wildflowers, past mountains that touched the sky, but then, something very strange happened. The donkey saw an angel standing in the road, with a shiny sword in his hand! The donkey was frightened and tried to move away from the scary figure.

But Balaam couldn't see the angel. He was puzzled and upset when the donkey wandered off the road, so he tried to steer her back. When she squeezed against a wall, crushing Balaam's foot, Balaam became frustrated and scolded the donkey. Then, the most extraordinary thing happened! The donkey turned to Balaam and said, "Why have you beaten me these three times? Haven't I always been a good donkey?" Balaam was speechless. His donkey was talking!

Before he could recover, God opened Balaam's eyes, and he saw the angel too. Balaam realized his donkey had saved him from danger, and he felt very sorry for his actions. He said to the angel, "I have sinned; I did not realize you stood against me. If I am wrong, I will go back."

The angel told Balaam to continue on his journey, but only to speak the words God would give him. Balaam, humbled and wiser, agreed. From that day forward, he listened more carefully to what God wanted him to say and do.

Now, dear little ones, Balaam's donkey teaches us that sometimes, lessons can come from unexpected places. Just like Balaam learned from his donkey, we should be open to learning from everyone around us. Even when things don't go our way, we should be patient and try to understand why. And remember, just like the donkey helped Balaam see the angel, sometimes God uses surprising ways to show us the right path. So, keep your hearts open, your minds curious, and your eyes wide for all the lessons this wonderful world has to teach!

Elijah and the Ravens

1 Kings 17:1-6

In a land full of olive trees and sandy dunes, there lived a brave man named Elijah. Elijah was a prophet, which means he listened to God and shared His words with others.

One day, God told Elijah that there would be no rain for a while, not until Elijah said so. This made life difficult because without rain, there were no crops, and without crops, there was little food.

God then told Elijah to go to a place called Kerith Ravine, east of the Jordan. "You will drink from the brook, and I have directed the ravens to supply you with food there," God said. Trusting God, Elijah packed his bag and set off for the journey.

When Elijah reached Kerith Ravine, he found a brook with crystal-clear water. He was just wondering about the food when he heard a soft cawing sound above him. He looked up and saw a group of black-feathered ravens, flying down from the blue sky.

To Elijah's surprise, each raven carried food in its beak! They had brought bread in the morning and meat in the evening, just like God had promised. Elijah was grateful. Each day, the ravens would come, bringing him food, and Elijah never went hungry.

Despite the hard times, Elijah was safe and fed, thanks to the ravens. He learned that no matter what, God would always take care of him.

Elijah and the helpful ravens teach us an important lesson about trust. Just as Elijah trusted God to take care of him, we can trust that God will take care of us too. Even when things seem tough or scary, remember that God loves you and He will always provide for you. So, hold onto your faith, be brave like Elijah, and always remember, even when it doesn't rain, God's love will always pour down on you.

Jesus Walks On Water

Matthew 14:22-33

Once upon a time, on a twinkling star-filled night, Jesus' friends, the disciples, were sailing on a big, beautiful boat on the Sea of Galilee. As the cool wind whooshed and the waves danced, Jesus wasn't with them. He had stayed behind to pray alone on a peaceful hill.
Suddenly, the wind grew stronger! Whoosh! Whoosh! The boat started to rock back and forth. The disciples were afraid, their eyes wide and hearts racing.

Then, in the middle of all the wind and waves, they saw something amazing. It was Jesus, walking on the water, coming towards them! But they didn't know it was Jesus. They thought it was a ghost and they were even more scared.

Just then, they heard a calm and gentle voice say, "Take courage! It's me. Don't be afraid." It was Jesus! His voice sounded like the softest lullaby.
Peter, one of the disciples, called out, "Lord, if it's really you, let me come to you on the water." Jesus replied, "Come." Filled with excitement and a sprinkle of fear, Peter stepped out of the boat and onto the water.

For a moment, Peter walked on water too! But then he saw the big waves and felt the strong wind. He got scared and started to sink. "Lord, save me!" he cried out.

Immediately, Jesus stretched out his hand and caught Peter. "Why did you doubt?" Jesus asked, as they climbed back into the boat.
As soon as they were safe in the boat, the wind stopped, and everything became peaceful. The disciples were amazed and said, "Truly, you are the Son of God."

Just like Jesus was there to help Peter when he was scared, Jesus is always with us too. He's there when you're scared of the dark, or when a storm thunders outside. Whenever you feel afraid, remember to have faith like Peter did. And always remember, Jesus is there to hold your hand, help you, and make the scary things go away. He loves you very, very much!

The Prodigal Son

Luke 15:11-32

In a sunny land filled with green fields and chirping birds, there lived a kind father with his two sons. The younger son, who was as playful as a young puppy, decided one day that he wanted his share of his father's money. He wished to explore the world, to see the towering mountains and shimmering seas!

With a heavy heart, the father divided his money. The younger son packed his bag and set off, waving goodbye. He traveled far and wide, spending his money on sweets and toys, and having big, fun parties with his new friends. But soon, his money ran out. No money meant no food, and no friends. His tummy rumbled louder than a thunderstorm, and he felt lonelier than a star in the sky.

In his deep hunger, he found a job feeding pigs. He was so hungry that the pigs' food started to look tasty! One day, as he watched the pigs munching, a thought sprouted in his mind like a seed in the ground. "Even my father's servants have more food than they can eat," he thought. "I will go back to my father."

With his heart pounding like a drum, he walked back home. He practiced his apology along the way, "Father, I have been silly and I'm sorry."
Seeing him from afar, his father's face brightened like the morning sun. He ran to his son, hugging him tightly. He was overjoyed, happier than a king with a new crown. He called his servants, "Prepare a big feast! My son has returned!"

The older brother was confused. Why was there a party for his brother who had been so thoughtless? The father gently explained, "Your brother was lost and now he's found. He made a mistake, but he's back now. And that's a reason to celebrate!"

But it's never too late to say you're sorry and make things right. And remember, like the father in the story, God's love for us is so big and so wide, He always welcomes us back with open arms.

Adam and Eve

Genesis 2-3

In the beginning, when the world was brand new, there was a garden filled with beautiful flowers of every color, singing birds of every size, and towering trees bearing juicy fruits. This garden was called Eden, a special place God had created.

In this lively garden, God made the first man, Adam, from the dust of the ground. Adam was alone for a short time. God created a friend for him, Eve, so that they could share the joys of Eden together.

God said, "You may eat from any tree in the garden, except for one - the Tree of Knowledge of Good and Evil. You mustn't eat its fruit or touch it." Adam and Eve promised to follow God's rule.

But one day, a sneaky serpent, slithering like a long, winding river, spoke to Eve. He tricked her, saying, "If you eat the fruit, you'll be just like God." Believing the serpent, Eve plucked a shiny, sweet-smelling fruit from the forbidden tree and shared it with Adam. They both took a big bite. Crunch! Suddenly, they realized they had done something they were not supposed to do. They felt so guilty, like a child who had secretly eaten an extra cookie before dinner. When God found out what they did, He was disappointed.

God said, "Because you didn't listen to my rule, you must leave the beautiful Garden of Eden." God still loved Adam and Eve, but there were consequences for their actions. So, they had to leave their lovely home and learn to live in the world outside.

The story of Adam and Eve teaches us a very important lesson, little ones. When we are given rules, it's for our own good, and it's important to follow them. It's okay to be curious, but we should always think about our choices and understand the consequences. And remember, even when we make mistakes, God still loves us very much, just like how a parent still loves their child, even when they do something naughty.

Moses Parts the Sea

Exodus 14:10-31

A long, long time ago, Moses, a brave man chosen by God, led his people out of Egypt where they were not treated kindly. They wanted to reach a wonderful land God promised them. But there was one big problem — a huge, glistening sea stood in their way!

Behind them, dust clouds rose in the air. The mean Pharaoh had changed his mind and was coming with his soldiers to get them! The people were scared. Their hearts pounded like big bass drums, "Boom, Boom!" But Moses said, "Don't be afraid! Stand still and watch God's power to save us!" Then, God told Moses, "Raise your staff and stretch out your hand over the sea." Moses did just as God commanded. He raised his staff high in the sky, as tall as a giraffe's neck. Suddenly, a strong wind began to blow. Whoosh! It blew all night long.

And then, the most amazing thing happened! The giant sea split into two, leaving a dry path in the middle. The walls of water stood tall on both sides, like two big, blue jello walls. Moses and the people walked right through the middle of the sea on dry ground, their eyes wide with wonder!

When Pharaoh and his soldiers tried to follow them, God made the wheels of their chariots get stuck. As soon as Moses and all the people were safe on the other side, God told Moses, "Stretch out your hand over the sea again." So, Moses stretched out his hand, and WHOOSH! The water went back to its place, covering Pharaoh's soldiers. The mean Pharaoh could not hurt Moses' people anymore.

Everyone cheered! "Hooray for God!" They danced and sang, grateful for God's protection. They knew that God was powerful and always with them, ready to help in the scariest of times.

Just like God helped Moses and his people, He is always there to help you too. Even when things look as big and impossible as parting a sea, God can make a way. So, whenever you're scared or in trouble, trust in God's mighty power and His big love for you!

The Last Supper

Luke 22:7-20

In the golden city of Jerusalem, Jesus decided to have a very special dinner. It was Passover, a big holiday like Christmas, and Jesus wanted to spend it with His best friends, the twelve disciples.

Jesus and His friends gathered around a large, wooden table. The table was full of yummy food: warm, fluffy bread, and a cup of sweet, red grape juice. The room was cozy, the candles twinkled like little stars, and the air was filled with love and friendship.

Jesus picked up a piece of bread, just as soft as a cloud. He thanked God for it, broke it into pieces, and shared it with His friends. "This bread is like my body," He said, "which I'm giving for you. When you eat it, remember me." The disciples, their eyes round as buttons, listened carefully.

Then, Jesus took the cup of grape juice. Its color was as rich as a sunset. He thanked God for it too and shared it with His friends. "This cup is like my blood," He said, "which is poured out for you. When you drink it, remember me." The disciples listened and understood. This was not just any dinner; it was a special way to remember Jesus' love for them.

From then on, every time they ate bread and drank from the cup, they remembered Jesus, His love, and His sacrifice. And today, when we do the same, we remember Jesus too, just like the disciples did at that special dinner.

The story of the Last Supper teaches us about love and remembrance. It shows us that just like Jesus loved His friends, we should love each other. And when we remember someone's kindness, it's like that person is still with us. So, let's remember to show love and kindness, just like Jesus did.

Jesus and the Easter Story

In a town called Jerusalem, lived the kindest man named Jesus. He healed the sick, made the blind see, and filled people's hearts with love. But, some powerful people didn't understand Jesus and felt threatened by him.

One day, these people decided to do a very sad thing. They made Jesus carry a heavy wooden cross up a big hill. Jesus was very tired and hurt, but he bravely kept going, his heart full of love for all people, even those who were unkind to him.

At the top of the hill, Jesus was put on the cross. Even though he was in pain, Jesus thought of others. He asked his dear friend, John, to take care of his mother, Mary. And then, with a great big love in his heart, Jesus asked God to forgive the people who had hurt him. "Father, forgive them, for they do not know what they are doing," he said.

After that, Jesus closed his eyes and his spirit went up to heaven. Everyone who loved Jesus felt very, very sad. They took Jesus's body down from the cross and placed it in a tomb, a special room in a cave, and rolled a big stone to close the entrance.

Dear little ones, the story of Jesus's crucifixion is a hard one, but it's also a story of the greatest love. Jesus loved us so much, he was willing to give up everything. His story teaches us to love others, even when they're not kind to us.

And remember, the story doesn't end with sadness. After three days, something miraculous happened - but that's a story for another day. The important thing to understand is that love is powerful and strong, just like Jesus's love for us. So, let's try to love like Jesus, being kind, forgiving, and caring to everyone we meet.